Magical Illusions:
Simple Tricks You Can Do!

written by Michael Teitelbaum

illustrated by Jared Lee

**McGraw-Hill
School Division**

New York   Farmington

An illusion is something that seems to be one thing but is really something else. Here are some magical illusions. You can learn to do these within a few minutes. Magicians usually guard the secrets of their tricks. But you can share these with your friends.

The Broken Pencil

Take a clear glass. Fill it halfway with water. Put a pencil in the glass. Look at the pencil through the side of the glass. The top part of the pencil isn't connected to the bottom part! The truth is that the pencil is still whole. The water changes the way the pencil looks. In fact, the water bends light, not the pencil.

The Floating Finger

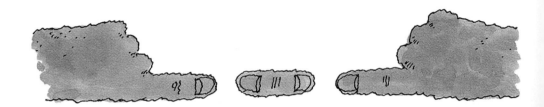

    Here's a trick your eyes and your brain play on you. Start by making a fist with each hand. Now straighten your index fingers (your index finger is next to your thumb) so they point at each other. The fingernails on your index fingers should be facing you. Your fingertips should almost be touching. Move your fingers about 1 to 2 inches in front of your nose. What do you see? Do you see a third, small finger floating in the air? And this finger has a fingernail at each end!

The illusion is created in your brain. Your brain combines pictures of both fingertips at once.

The Disappearing Pencil

This is a trick you can do for an audience. Sit at a table with a tablecloth on it. Hold a pencil in your right hand. Hold a cloth in your left. Cover the pencil with the cloth.

As you cover the pencil, use your index finger to hold up the cloth. To your audience, it will look like the pencil is holding up the cloth. Drop the pencil into your lap (you're behind the table, so no one will see the pencil fall). Now pull the cloth off. Presto! Your right hand is empty. You have created the illusion that the pencil has magically disappeared!

Banana Stretching

Here's one more trick played on you by your eyes and brain. Use this one to amaze your friends. Take two bananas that are the same length. Place banana 1 on a table. Pretend to stretch banana 2.

Then place it above banana 1. Make sure the stems line up. Banana 2 looks like it's longer. Now pick up banana 2 and pretend to squeeze it so that it shrinks. This time, place banana 2 below banana 1. Banana 2 looks like it's smaller! You have created the illusion that the bananas changed sizes. The top banana will always look longer. It is just a bit closer to your eyes.

Hole in Your Hand

Your eyes can play tricks on you. Some of them can be really creepy! Take a piece of paper. Roll it into a tube. Hold the tube in your left hand. Put it up to your left eye. Hold up your right hand with your palm facing toward you. Place your right hand next to the tube. Make sure they touch. Look through the tube with your left eye. Keep your right eye open. Your eyes and brain create the illusion that there is a hole in your right hand!

Your brain combines what your left eye sees
and what your right eye sees into one picture.

The Vanishing Penny

In this trick you will create the illusion that you made a penny vanish. Before you begin, place a penny in the palm of your left hand. Then place a clear glass containing a small amount of water over the penny. It will look like the penny is in the glass. Show the glass and penny to your friend. Say that you have a penny in a glass.

Now cover the glass with a cloth. Hand
the covered glass to your friend like a gift.
As you do this, close your left hand around
the penny. Ask your friend to remove the
cloth. Magically, the penny has vanished!

Royal Illusion

The last trick once again uses your eyes and your brain to create an illusion. Ask your friends to stare at this picture for one full minute. Then ask your friends to stare at a blank wall for another minute. Magically, the image of a red king with black eyes will appear before them!

Want to Learn More?

If you are interested in learning how to do more magic tricks, look for magic trick books at your public library. Here are some titles of books to help you get started:

Amazing Magic Tricks
by Dave Brown and Paul Reeve
DK Publishing, 1995

This book introduces 30 classic magic tricks. Step-by-step photos show the reader how to perform the tricks.

Magic
by Peter Eldin

This book gives an overview of famous magic tricks throughout the ages. It includes an A–Z guide to the world's greatest magicians.

A Magician
by Ivan Bulloch and Diane James
World Book Inc., 1997

Useful tips for magicians on what to do, what to wear, and how to put on a magic show.

Science Magic Tricks
by Nathan Shalit, illustrated by Helen Ulan

Dozens of magic tricks based on optical illusions, mathematics, and magnetism.